TAKE This booK

bend the

I0617263

page corners

crease & crinkle the pages

bend the spine

READ IT ANY AND
EVERYWHERE

It's as portable
as your phone.

YES!

YOU NEED YOUR PHONE

(even while you read!)

This book consist of QR codes, to be scanned with your phone camera. Once scanned, you gain access to

so much more

than just a book.

"EVERY TWEEN AND TEENAGER IN AMERICA NEEDS THIS BOOK"

ISBN: 979-8-9909568-3-4

WHY DOES EVERY TWEEN AND TEENAGER IN AMERICA NEED THIS BOOK?

It's simple: this book carries timeless value every young person needs to know.

That probably sounds stereotypical of most self-help books, but as a young person, (only **13** !) I can confirm it's true.

I wrote this book while I was **13**, or as I call it, during Year **13**. Year **13** was my year, just not the year I expected. I had my first encounter with the "real world" and it made me question everything. Most importantly, people.

aRE pEopLE EvEN WoRTh iT?

AM I
WORTH
IT?

Why did it fail?

Why did people not
support me?

WHAT DID
I DO
WRONG?

am i just a little kid?

I pondered these questions during the majority of **2024**.

Did I make it to the end of the tunnel I call Year **13**? You'll have to find out.

PROVE THE ADULTS WRONG

I must be *that* teen ...

What teenager receives a business as a birthday gift?

What teen takes failure and finds new hope?

I MUST BE SPECIAL. AND YOU ARE, TOO

Being special has nothing to do with social class, money and who your parents are.

RiGhT?

I've been knocked down but I'm sticking to my belief that everybody is special, unique and talented. Remove all other stigmas, notions and past ideas of those words.

YOU ARE *that* teen regardless of social class, money and who your parents are.

WARNING

WARNING

WARNING

WARNING

THIS BOOK CHRONICLES THE DEEP THOUGHTS AND OPINIONS OF A 13 year old  girl

CONTENTS OF
MY THOUGHTS

The meaning of the age 13 has a tight grip on our society.

I never could understand why so many people put emphasis on a 1 & a 3 standing next to each other.

It did not seem different from when a 1 and another 1 were together. {Insert Heavy Sigh Here} I was wrong.

Turning 13 is definitely worth the hype, especially when you know so much for your age. I'm not saying I'm 13 GoiNG oN 30, but my mental and physical age are not in sync.

That's the only explanation, for what 13 year old writes a book chronicling the lessons she has learned on her quest to become a successful teen?

I wrote this book because I never want another youth who is trying to be good feel defeated when their efforts are not recognized.

Loud
Silence
offer concrete hope to
received their shots longer
cases, we found that vaccinated peo

Loud Silence is a term I coined when I realized how unsupportive the world can be. I recorded this voice note in December 2023, the same month my business closed.

my voice note

Scan with your phone camera to listen

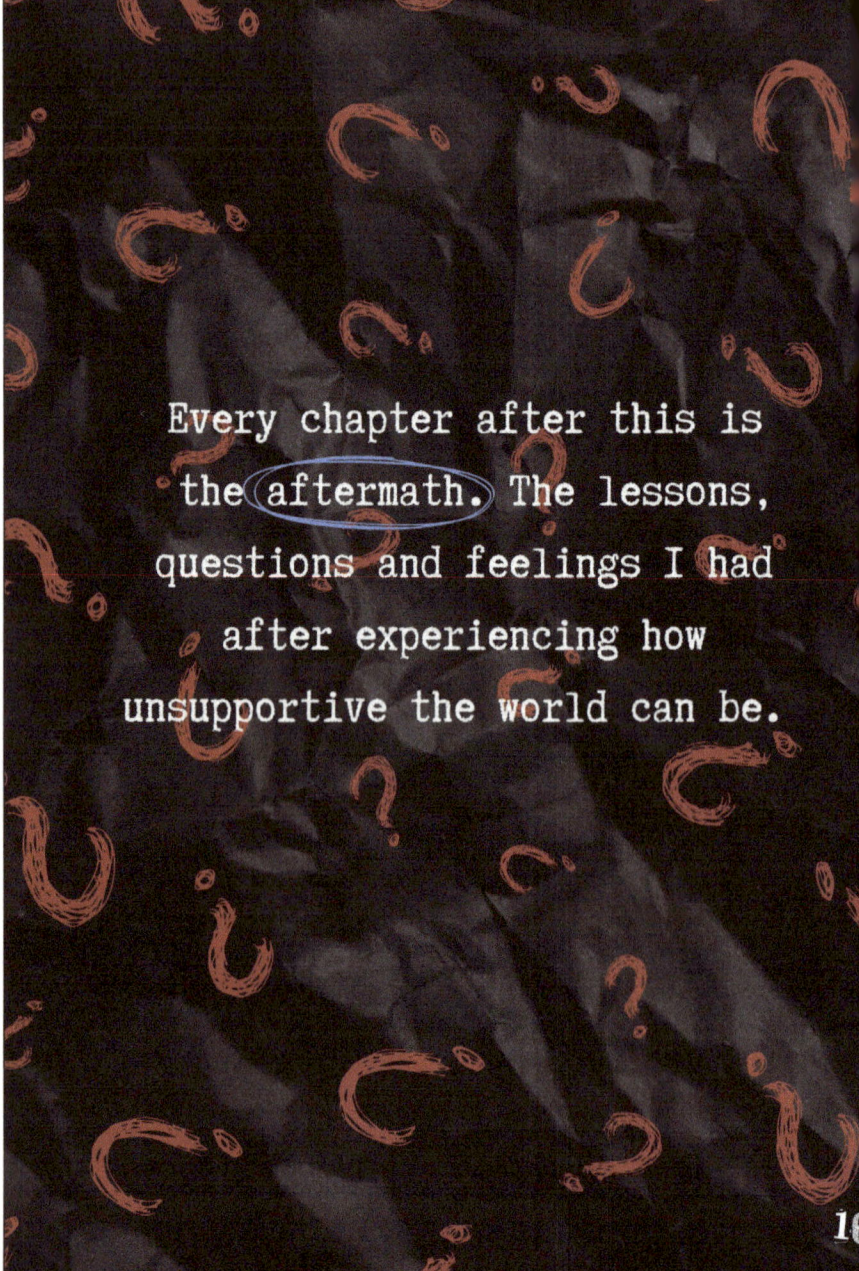

Every chapter after this is the (aftermath.) The lessons, questions and feelings I had after experiencing how unsupportive the world can be.

Bittersweet

The older I get, the more I realize how unfair success can be. As someone who wants to achieve massive levels of success, I find myself pondering many different questions.

what makes a person more successful than another?

HOW ARE MASSIVE AMOUNTS OF SUCCESS ACCUMULATED?

WhAT doEs ThE WoRd sUCCEss TRuLY MEAN?

These questions float around my mind at all times of the day. While I do not have an answer to them, I do have a word I use to describe the emotion I feel about the disparity of success: Bittersweet. I have felt this emotion more in the past year, than ever before. However, my mind is not clouded black by this emotion, instead a golden string of hope and ambition is born. A form of success I wish to accumulate is an established personal brand with strong fanbase of individuals who I inspire and uplift and will support my creative endeavors. As the internet and social media has risen, so has content creators, the people that supply the content people know and love. Over the past few years, thousands, perhaps millions of people have decided to become content creators. Showcasing a talent, skill, product, pet, business and even their own lives on social media in hopes of turning views into paychecks. A wonderful concept, really.

However, I can't help but notice the productivity and substance lack from some videos. I notice the videos which collect millions of views are sometimes the videos that provide the most useless content. Another observation is how videos of value are not thought of as valuable from the public. I notice it almost mimics a switch: invaluable content gains the most recognition while the valuable content collects dust in a corner. It saddens, even worries me. How can I, someone who desires to add value to society, be seen as valuable by society? By my observations, I have sincere doubts. Ultimately, this leads to my bittersweet emotion. I see people establish personal brands that are not truly personal at all, only fabricated tales. Or perhaps the personal brand is truly personal, but unproductive, showcasing behaviors better left unrecorded.

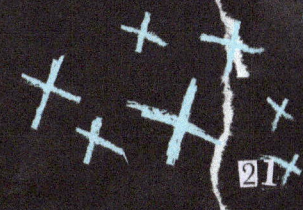

i want to create productive content, but how can i in a world that favors unproductive content?

While a social media content creator and a brick-and-mortar business owner operate in different worlds, the public reaction exist in both. When I had my brick- and-mortar business, it was malnourished of support, leading to its grave. However, while it was alive, I noticed how parents still preferred other businesses, rather than my productive, youth focused one. While I understand parents have priorities and some households cannot afford extracurriculars, some off my events were free. I decided to alter my entire business plan to provide free, productive events to give the youth tools to succeed and explore in a creative space. It still puzzles me why people didn't support. People will support an overpriced cookie shop but not an affordable, productive place for their kids. The same principle applies for why a thirty second baking video garners more views than a person supplying people with knowledge to help them succeed.

the attention society gives to certain type of content, businesses and people is so uneven it makes me wonder the end goal.

Why even have an end goal? Why strive for perfection when mediocre is rewarded top marks? Why mold yourself into a productive, positive person when negativity and unproductiveness wins?

All of these thoughts fizzle about in my mind, leading to one final statement to be the cherry-on-top:

It's so sweet to see the success of others, but I'm met with a bitter aftertaste of wondering why my productiveness and talents are not garnering the same recognition.

I'm

hAPPY FoR oThERs;

why can't others

bE hAPPY FoR ME?

Every parent wants their child to succeed. As kids, even as teenagers, we are told,

"The world is yours" or "I wish I could give you the world".

My parents used similar phrases from time to time, but the one liner my parents said stuck out to me the most:

"NO ONE CARES THAT YOUR NAME IS HALEE"

I've been hearing the phrase since I was 5 years old. Sometimes my father said it with solemn, sometimes my mother said it when life showed us how true the phrase was.

The line echoed in my mind like a boomerang, bouncing back and forth between my ears around the time my brick and mortar business was closing. That was the first time when I realized how true the phrase was. In the window of my business, I proudly declared it was owned by Halee.

Perhaps that's the reason why you sometimes never know the names behind your favorite billion dollar brands.

No one cares.

Saying it out loud as I write this is spine tingling, but it's the truth.

My parents provided a delicate balance of encouraging my dreams while also addressing the fact that no one will support me "just cause". The second part is my motivation to ensure every act I do has substance and purpose.

NOTHING IS A COINCIDENCE OR "JUST CAUSE".

WHAT IF THERE WAS A DIFFERENT PERSPECTIVE?

What if we are grouping the "one" in NOC with multiple people?

no one cares

For me, when I say No One Cares, I really mean They Don't Care. The "they" being outsiders, people I want to follow my accounts on social media, people I want to buy my books, people I want to write nice reviews.

Perhaps the sadder truth in this chapter is the "they" (who ever they might be) have a lot of power, despite class and financial status. The "they" can control how people view you, your business or whatever project you want support on. "They" can control how you view yourself and your worth.

Who's YouR "ThEY"?

SO...

I want to tell you this,
because your parents might not.

The world is your oyster,
the people are not. You
can do anything, you can't
make people do anything.
Did you catch it? It's
okay, it'll come back to
you like a boomerang.

make noise,
not mess

SCREAM FROM THE ROOFTOPS!

Shout Loud AND pRoud!

About what? Latest celebrity news(really gossip)? About the tutor who helped the McAllen family's kids improve their grades? About how little Benny opened a lemonade stand and dreams of seeing his drink in a store?

What is worthy of our attention these days? Are you worthy of attention? What type of attention? Do you even want attention? Do you think the people and topics we give attention to are worthy?

it's the middle of the afternoon and of course these questions are banging in my brain.

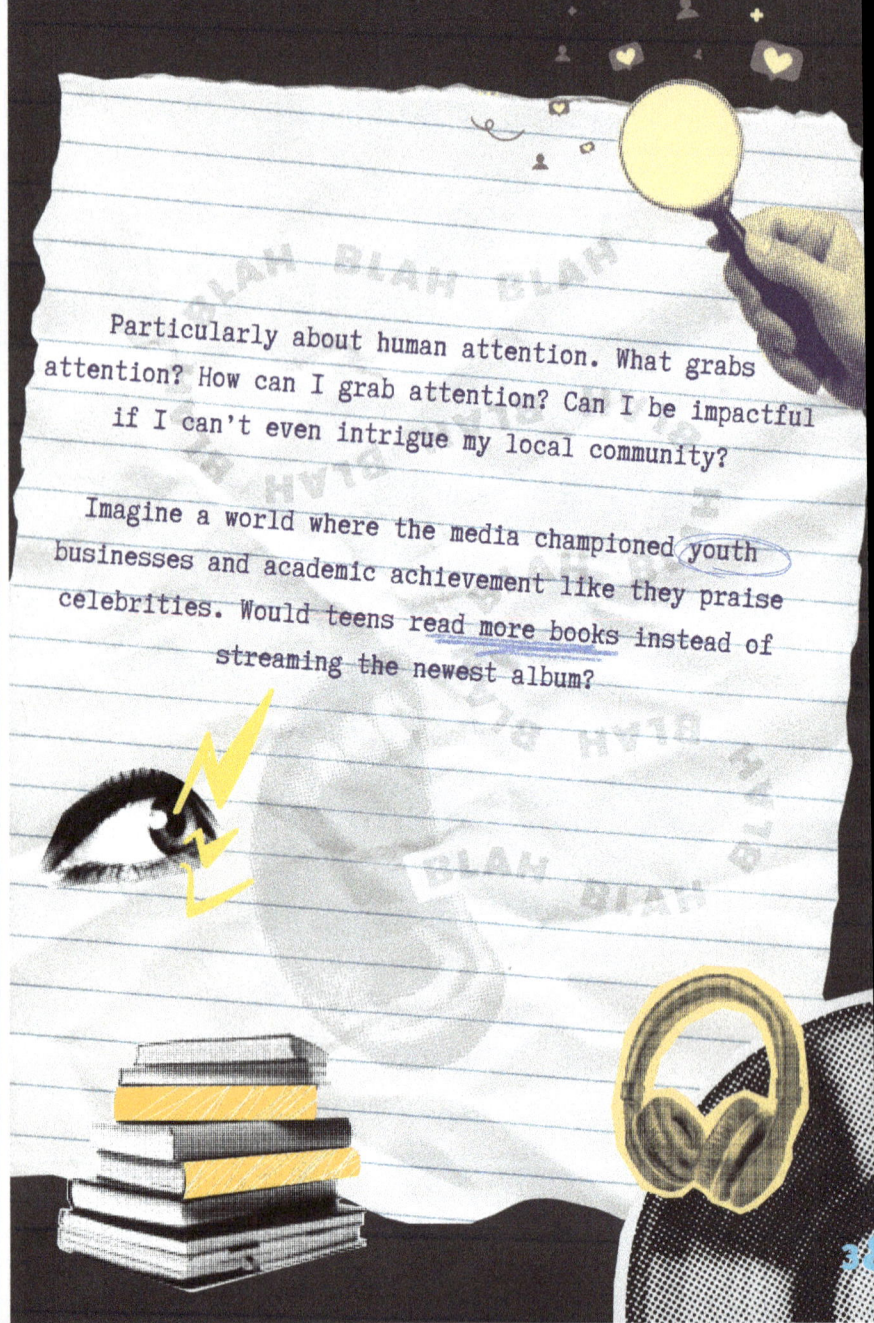

Particularly about human attention. What grabs attention? How can I grab attention? Can I be impactful if I can't even intrigue my local community?

Imagine a world where the media championed youth businesses and academic achievement like they praise celebrities. Would teens read more books instead of streaming the newest album?

I remember an encounter at my brick-and-mortar business, it was the first time people had walked through the doors since my grand opening. For context, my business was two feet away from a dance studio. The Dance Studio was most active in the evening, when the Dance Moms would drop off their daughters and afterwards chat in front of my business and the Dance Studio.

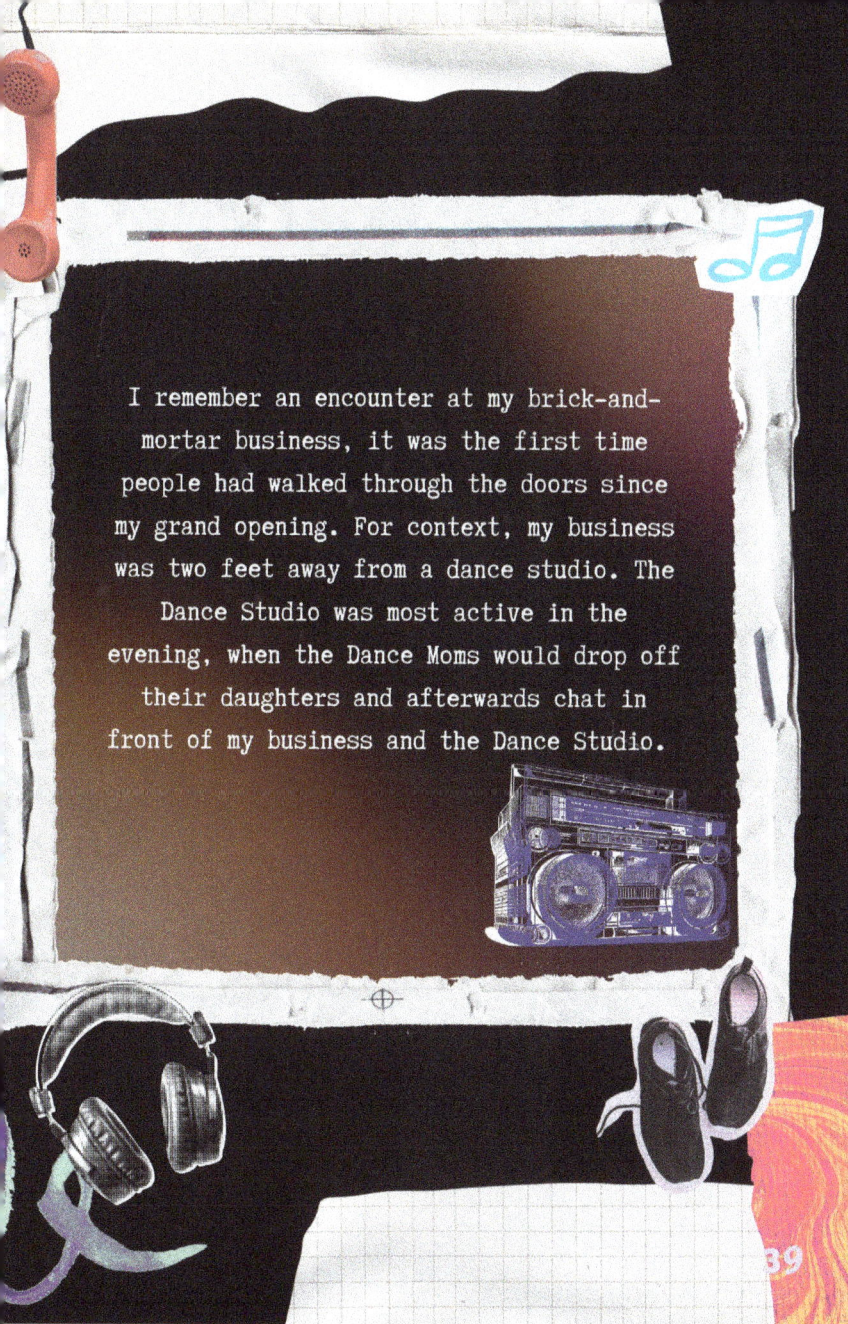

One day, three of the Dance Moms walked in and started asking what type of business I had. At first, they directed the questions to my mother, who gladly motioned for me to answer. I then introduced the concept, gave them a tour and promoted upcoming events and programs we offered.

I was overjoyed a group of people decided to enter my business I didn't realize something.

they didn't take me seriously

In fact one even joked about a spot for adults after I explained the concept was for a youth entertainment space and after school program.

HAVE YOU EVER FELT LIKE PEOPLE DON'T GET YOU?

4

At dinner time the same day, my parents explained and dissected the encounter. They didn't mean to deflate my enthusiasm, **it just happened.**

I SAID THE RIGHT WORDS TO THE WRONG PEOPLE.

I vow never again.

the encounter of the dance moms brought me to a realization and a question:

If you remember anything from this book, please let it be the fact that your words, time, talent and skills are valuable, never let people treat or tell you otherwise.

(I think that might be the most powerful sentence I have ever written)

I used to get overly excited and just accept. Mainly because I wanted people to notice, so I entertained every interaction. I never judged, because I thought my value and positivity would infect others.

When I was nine, at brick and mortar school for the first time, I was thrilled at the opportunity to make friends. However I 'befriended' people I'm not even sure wanted to be my friend. The encounter with the Dance Moms is similar and now I'm glad they were never my customers. I know the value my business could have brought to the community, yet when people are content, no force can make them evolve.

GROWING UP, I WAS TAUGHT:

- don't gossip
- don't lie
- don't be messy

In other words, don't be a Noisy Nelly. In my small circle of people, my parents taught me how to observe and detect the Noisy Nellies of the world. The people who thrived on hearing the latest and feasted on negativity. Most importantly, the people who shouted the gossip, dare I say mess, from the rooftops. In the age of social media, communities of Noisy Nellys gather and feast together as they gossip and tear people down.

The encounter with the Dance Moms was some day in October, weeks after my business had been open to the public and months since my family first started renovating it. The girl back then did not question why the sudden intrusion, but I now know it was the Noisy Nellies in the flesh. Three of them bold enough to try to add truth to their rumors. The comments of what I thought they would say about me would constantly occupy my mind.

DON'T MAKE MY MISTAKE. YOUR MIND IS A DIAMOND, NEVER LET IT WONDER ABOUT RHINESTONES.

diamonds

vs

rhinestones

I love to talk. I don't have a lot of friends, so I mainly have conversations with my parents about my goals and plans. When my business first opened, I was thrilled to tell people the impact I wanted to have. Anybody who listened, I would open my mouth and speak to.

I remember one day in late August or early September, I met the Principal of the local middle school. It was thrilling, I met with one person who then called the Principal to schedule the meeting. I felt like a true business woman, dashing from one meeting to another. I felt like I was accomplishing something. In the car, my mother and I discussed speaking points. When we arrived, we were directed to the Principal's office

THIS IS MY CHANCE,

I thought.

The person who arranged the meeting briefed the Principal of the programs and activities my business offered. After introductions were given, my mother and I started pitching the programs. I presented my pitch with bright eyes and enthusiasm. My mother detected the disinterest before me, yet I still kept talking. The moment I realized the Principal was disinterested, was when I handed her the flyer for a program and she glanced down and shoved it back. My mother told her the copy was for her to keep. Anxiety and doubt crept on me, and I desperately tried to win her interest back, thinking my pitch was wrong.

LONG STORY SHORT, THE PRINCIPAL NEVER WORKED WITH MY BUSINESS. I WALKED OUT OF THE SCHOOL FEELING DEFEATED AND WONDERING WHAT I SAID WRONG.

Remember last chapter when I wrote,

"your mind is a diamond, never let it wonder about rhinestones"

The moment with the Principal is a perfect example. I went into the school with a pitch, talking points and enthusiasm. I left wondering if my business could do any good for the community. That wasn't the first time I opened my mouth to the wrong people. During the time of trying to get customers, I met people who were shocked a child could speak so well but ultimately did not support or understand my business.

I know now everybody who enters your life is not the people you need to discuss ideas and try to collaborate with. I also learned everybody who talks good game does not play a good game.

I never thought it was good to be one of those people who were reserved and who only talked to people with certain status symbols (fancy cars, nice purses, etc). I thought a good conversation and opportunity could come from any one, regardless of their appearance. I knew I didn't have all of the flashy symbols yet, but I wanted people to take me seriously and as a credible source.

Many encounters and wrong conversations later, I confidently inform you the approach of being reserved can work. I'm not saying only talk to the rich, but read social cues and act accordingly. Like my parents always tell me, "Read the room, Halee". I'm reading the room, underlying social cues and drawing conclusions from them. You should too. After all you can bring value and you are valuable. Not every environment is right for you and that's okay.

BREAK
THRU
STONE

55'

WHEN PEOPLE ARE CONTENT, NO FORCE CAN MAKE THEM EVOLVE.

5

An August summer day, my father is at work and my mother and I are in the car completing errands. My father is questioning whether all the time, energy and money is necessary for the building renovations in order for the business to start generating funds. My mother firmly answers yes.

For context, my father operated his company during the day and spent his evenings and nights renovating the building, with occasional help from friends and relatives. It would be shameful to the landlord to display a 'before' picture of the building before my father worked his magic. Sincerely, magic was made because the building was painted bright yellow and green, had concrete floors, and a kitchen in desperate need of TLC.

Granted, the rent was extremely cheap, so my parents decided intense renovations were worth it, especially since profit was soon to follow.

If it hasn't been made clear, my business was a failure that taught me many lessons... and caused extreme guilt.

Guilt because my parents poured every resource into the building renovations and into the operation of the business, only to be met with silence. The goal was to create an environment to introduce youth to different skills such as graphic design, web design, public speaking, among other activities. My business was located in a small, undeprivelaged town. I could have placed my business in another town with more privileged kids, but I wanted to give back to an underserved community. Most people would have saw a rundown town with historical properties, but I saw a place with empty buildings ripe for positive establishments. If my business succeeded, I would've expanded and possibly opened a second business. I thought my new business off of Main Street could have attracted more businesses to see the unlocked potential of the town.

when my business closed in december of 2023, i blamed myself.

"i should've posted more on social media"

"i should've attended more pop up events"

"i should've talked to more people"

I know now the "should've's" would not have prevented the end, maybe delay it, but the ending was inevitable. In a way, I'm glad the venture ended in 2023, 2024 is my year to process. In the process of processing, I have drawn an important conclusion:

"when people are content, no force can make them evolve."

Nobody can change a person's mind when the mind is closed to new ideas. It's my version of the proverb:

" you can bring a horse to water but you can't make him drink"

61

I brought the water, fancy mineral water, but the people still chose other festivities. I even offered free events, to make my business accessible to everyone. When the glass crumbled and my parents moved out of the building, I looked around and realized:

I left the town the exact same as I found it,

but it's not my fault.

I tried, my parents used every resource they had, and it was more than enough. The people in that town are settled, their lives set in stone. When I told people the business concept, most were baffled.

A PLACE FOR KIDS RAN BY ONE? HOW ELEMENTARY.

I'm not sure if they thought the idea was extraordinary and out of reach or just plain silly.

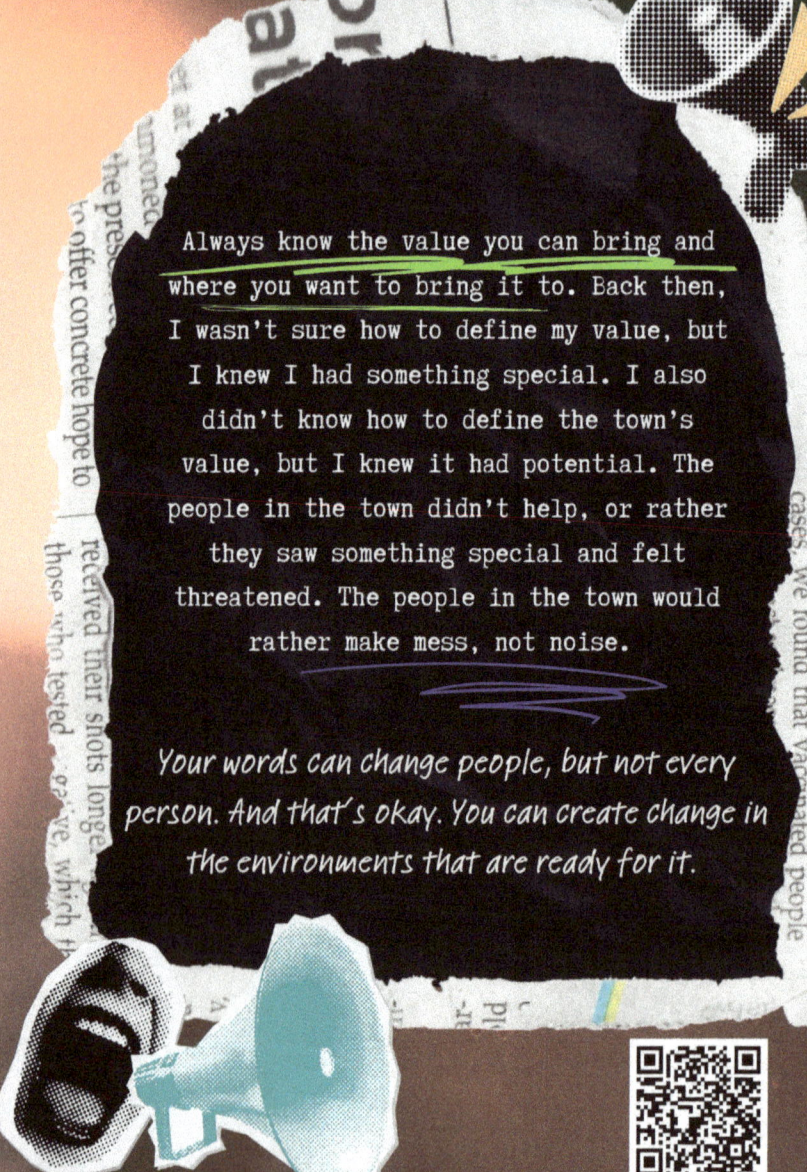

Always know the value you can bring and where you want to bring it to. Back then, I wasn't sure how to define my value, but I knew I had something special. I also didn't know how to define the town's value, but I knew it had potential. The people in the town didn't help, or rather they saw something special and felt threatened. The people in the town would rather make mess, not noise.

Your words can change people, but not every person. And that's okay. You can create change in the environments that are ready for it.

that teen

"i'm not special"

"What makes me unique?"

"i don't have talent"

Those phrases only float in your mind
because you haven't found YOU yet.

YOU bEiNG,
WeLL, yOu.
No fancy acronyms needed.

WHAT MAKES YOU FEEL ALIVE?
WHAT MAKES ENERGY FLOW
THROUGH YOUR VEINS?
WHAT MAKES YOU
WHOLEHEARTEDLY HAPPY?

Take time to get to know yourself.
Take time to find YOU.

Scan the QR code below to open a list of questions to help you get to know yourself.

How can you believe and have confidence in yourself if you don't know who you are?

It may take a few hours, it may take a few days, it may take few years but I wholeheartedly believe knowing your talents, skills, strengths and weaknesses are vital to become

that teen.

WHAT IS
that teen ?

A term I created in hopes of sparking a positive phenomenon among teenagers.

"i'm kidding, i'm kidding"

In all seriousness, **that** teen is exactly who it sounds like: **that** teen

 that teen you can't help but notice.

 that teen who knows their strengths, weaknesses, skills and talents.

*that teen who is working towards their goals in a positive manner.

that teen who knows how to communicate

For example, I discovered some of my talents and skills during childhood. I discovered my talent was writing at 7 years old. Since then, a slew of A+ essays and flattering comments from teachers followed. At age nine, my parents didn't let me waste my time on Youtube, instead they introduced me to graphic design platforms. I experimented with these platforms, then I became interested in video editing. At age 12, I entered my first short film contest, entering a video about the American Literacy Crisis, a topic I wrote an essay on. In middle school, I created many presentations and videos for my class assignments, each earning top marks from my teachers.

During the Pandemic, I slowly started to incorporate my skills and talents in my business. I began selling online courses, digital files, ebooks and tried to build an online community. In middle school, I created a membership community for tweens who want to explore graphic design, book clubs and writing workshops.

JULY 2023

My parents have a found a building with affordable rent. Coincidently, my birthday month is July, so instead of a designer bag, my parents gifted me a retail space to take my business from online to brick-and-mortar.

By now, you know the ending of that story. However, it's a great example of how I am ***that* teen.** I am fortunate enough to have found my talent and skills at an early age and have parents who encouraged me to make money with them. Ever since 2018-2019, my parents encouraged me to make videos and gain an audience online. To be honest, I used to regret not doing it and feeling bittersweet seeing other kid influencers become viral. However, I'm very glad I didn't starting building my platform back then. Not to sound cliche, but I'm still finding who I am. If I was consumed with making content at 8 years old, I never would have developed my talent for writing.

If social media had been my focus from young, my other skills and interest wouldn't have been developed. Is it bittersweet seeing kids around my age get brand deals and massive amounts of support just because they do funny skits? Yes. However, I'm glad my focus has always been about topics of substance. It has brought me to an important conclusion:

To be *that* teen, you need to be a READER, WRITER, THINKER, CREATOR, LEADER, SPEAKER, & PRESENTER.

For me, it all started with reading. As a kid I would read Nancy Clancy chapter books religiously. The more I read fiction, the more my mind wondered about creating my own characters and fantasies. Soon enough I was writing my own stories and my parents were searching for a publisher. A part of my school work was journaling for fifteen minutes a day. This simple framework laid the foundation for me to develop my writing skills. If you feel like your writing skills need a polish, definitely try it.

READER+
WRITER

You need to think. Plain and simple. A society that discourages thinking is a dangerous one. Everything a human does requires thinking, whether your realize it or not. Knowing how to understand what one person is saying is very imrptoant. Knowing how to think critically about a situation and find solutions are valuable skills.

Thinker

In the words of Einstein:
"creativity is intelligence having fun".
Creativity is whatever you make it.
Creativity shouldn't have boundaries or
be limited to a certain area.
However you like to create, do it.

CREATOR

I can proudly say I am the two-time, first female president of my school's
National Junior Honor Society. (I even have a medal!)
The job introduced me to leadership skills and taught me how to communicate and orchestrate a group of people. I was in charge of making presentations, assigning duties to the other officers, and hosting our monthly meetings. Not only will it look good on my college applications, but the role allowed me to learn how to manage and organize a large group.

An element to my career path is being a public speaker. However, even if you don't plan to be a public speaker, knowing how to communicate with people is important. I'm not just referring to your friends. You should know to speak to anyone and have effective communication skills. Cleary stating your point, being present in the conversation, not zoning out, are all examples of having effective communication.

SPEAKER

79

As previously stated, I create numerous presentations in middle school. You should know how to present information, whether it's verbally or visually. For example, you want to persuade your parents to let you become a content creator. Your parents may offer push back, so you need to know how present your point and address your parents concerns.

Presenter

All of these are examples of how reading, writing, thinking, creating, leading, speaking and presenting has impacted my life. While your aspirations may be different from mine, these skills are beneficial for anyone.

Do you like watching funny videos on social media, then scrolling through the comments for a greater laugh? Me too! I also consider it flexing my reading skills.

My favorite comments are the ones where people debate the video topic. The people wh type their long, drawn out explanations ar using their writing skills.

READERS
WRITERS
THINKERS
CREATORS
LEADERS
SPEAKERS
PRESENTERS
are everywhere.

Scan with your phone camera

Freedom

8

WHAT IS FREEDOM?

I've heard about it on TV. People have traveled over seas to foreign lands and started wars for it. Teenagers in sitcoms rebelled against their parents for a taste of "freedom".

For me, life is about freedom. The freedom to choose the life path I want. The freedom to choose how much I want to make in an hour. The freedom of having choices.

DO YOU GET TO HAVE CHOICES?

When I was around four years old, my parents asked me what color I wanted to paint my room. I chose blue. Not a navy blue, not a pale blue, but a sky blue. It was bright, it was cheerful. I still regard the bright blue color as the color of my childhood. However, I really wanted purple. A nice deep, cheerful purple because my all time favorite TV character was Doc Mcstuffins. Yet, I was a swept away by the Frozen craze.

MORAL OF THE STORY: PURPLE SHOULD'VE WON AND DON'T LET HYPE CLOUD YOUR MIND.

The real reason I just shared that story was to tell you I've always had choices. 8

The Yves Saint Laurent campaign of Dua Lipa declaring freedom is permanently etched into my brain. The way Dua Lipa openly declares freedom with a falcon on her wrist is the type of freedom we should all aspire to. We should all aspire to announce our freedom in such a vibrant and reckless manner, with an exotic pet donned next to us.

While I know this was all a marketing ploy for YSL's product, I couldn't but draw conclusions to what freedom is in my brain.

For me, freedom is choices. While most adults expect this impulse of freedom from teenagers, this impulse surges deeper than the depths of a suburban high school.

Freedom is not having to accept a standard of something because another human says it's all they deserve. That's my freedom.

FREE**do**M **is:**

NOT HAVING
LIMITATIONS

Yet, preparing for this life is something that should start during those years. I know the kind of life I want, I know I want to live freely, I just need to get there.

8

HALEE'S OFFICIAL LIST OF FREEDOM

- Saying "no" to opportunities that don't suit you

- The ability to travel whenever

- The freedom to only be in environments that align and are safe

- Blessing the less fortunate

- Never comprising on your whole hearted dreams

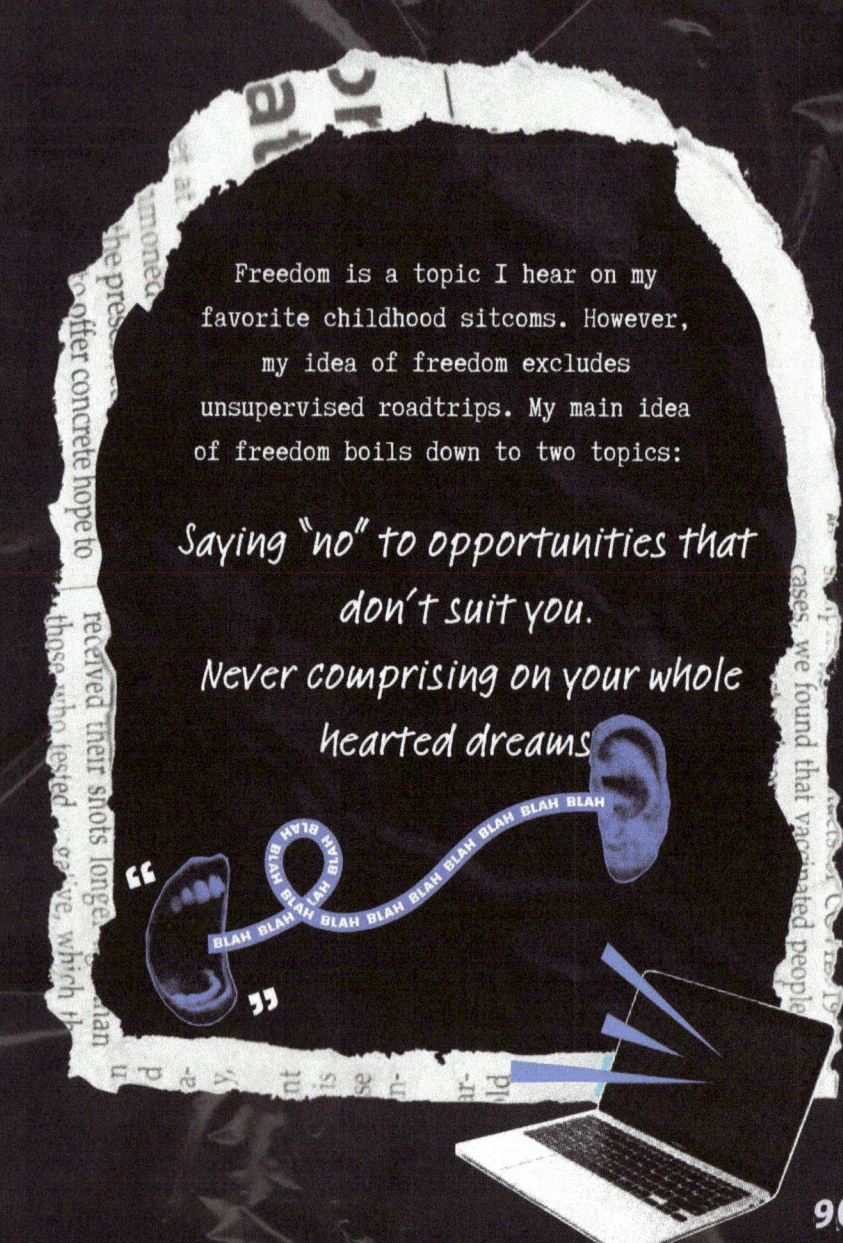

Freedom is a topic I hear on my
favorite childhood sitcoms. However,
my idea of freedom excludes
unsupervised roadtrips. My main idea
of freedom boils down to two topics:

Saying "no" to opportunities that
don't suit you.
Never comprising on your whole
hearted dreams

BLAH BLAH BLAH BLAH BLAH BLAH BLAH BLAH BLAH BLAH

With wealth comes freedom. I believe this entirely. However, your idea of freedom and mine may differ, so you may disagree. My idea of freedom is listed on the previous pages. which for me requires wealth. However, I can exercise my freedom now. The ability to say "no" is one we all have, however when you are the underdog, every opportunity can seem like gold. As mentioned is the previous chapters, I reacted the same way and exchanged valuable information with invaluable people. Saying "no" comes from a place of security and self confidence in your abilities, something wealth cannot buy.

WHAT'S YOUR FREEDOM ??!?!!?!

only for you

Ever since I was around 11 years old, Stanford was my dream university.

In Early 2023, I took time to research and ponder my future career. In fact, I spent a whole week researching Stanford and making plans for the courses I wanted to take. I soon became caught in a draw between choosing law, neuroscience or immunology.

In the midst of the battle, I also started viewing videos on social media of women in the law field. I was hoping to gain more insight on a possible career path. The testimonies I found of women included sexism, racism and overall poor human treatment.

I researched more testimonies and
made a bold conclusion:

i never want to work for anyone.

i never want to compromise my dream
to work for someone else's success.

i never want to be forty years old and
wonder what could've been.

I never want to one day be
the mature adult in a room
full of hopeful teenagers
decades later saying,

"I COULD'VE BEEN THE
HIT PODCASTER.
I COULD'VE BEEN THE
BEST SELLING AUTHOR.
I COULD'VE BEEN A
PHILANTHROPIST."

The idea of jumping through hoops and plowing through ringers to earn a spot, is agitating to me.

Well, let me rephrase that,

jumping through hoops and plowing through ringers to earn a spot somewhere that does not completely align with me, is agitating.

WHY GO THROUGH ALL THAT IF NOT FOR YOUR DREAM?

The path I'm taking has potholes and hoops to jump through, but it's the path I chose. It's the path I'm passionate about.

The idea of being an immunologist is fun. I love to dream of a clinic painted bright teal with a smiling receptionist and parents to inform about their children's allergies. Standing up for justice and presenting the case in a courtroom leaves a thrill down my spine. Becoming a cognitive neuroscientist would honor my ten your old self completely.

HOWEVER, THE WHAT IF'S AND 'WHAT COULD'VE BEEN' WILL STAY IMPRINTED IN MY MIND.

I'm not against college.

I'm against striving to achieve something that isn't entirely you.

Intense studying, anxiety about grades, unknown campuses are not entirely worth it to reach an end goal that does not entirely align with me. Perhaps my outlook has been shaped from some of my middle school experiences. In sixth and seventh grade, I was the ultimate overachiever. The longer essays, carefully constructed presentations did not seem like overachieving to me, but it was. My teachers left flattering comments, but even with the extra work I put it, it was just middle school, not my future career. I became riddled with headaches, anxiety and was stressed trying to be the 'best'.

In reality, I should've tried my hardest but not push my limits to the point of exhaustion. I'm proud of the work I put out, but it wasn't worth the stress and anxiety that clouded me. **I overextended myself.**

In so many ways, I craved academic validation. Instead, I needed to know an A+ on a school paper did not guarantee an A+ in life. Granted, my parents had these conversations and tried redirect me. However, my experience with trying to gain customers for my business opened my eyes to how little people can care about academics. My mentions of being a published author (I self-published my first chapter book in 2022 prior with Amazon KDP) were glazed over with little to no consideration. The people in the town didn't care about A's I received on English papers or how active I participated in my live virtual classes. The fact I was president of my school's NJHS did not matter.

I'm never going to stop trying my hardest in school, and you shouldn't either. However, never overextend yourself if it isn't worth it. Only overextend yourself for you, your dreams, your plans, and your goals.

(JUST MAKE SURE YOU GIVE 100% TO EVERYTHING ELSE)

for your clarity

DO NOT SLACK!

This chapter is not your excuse to leave homework, household chores and other responsibilities undone. I have learned to give my best work to all of my responsibilities without draining myself. I still strive to make a good grade in English, but I'm not trying to write ten extra pages when the assignment was to write two. I'm encouraging you to know your limits and try hard without burning yourself out.

Me, Myself and I

whole heart

I am powerful
I am capable
I am brilliant

In the last chapter, I talked about how difficult it would be for me to live with myself if I didn't choose a life path I whole heartedly wanted. In a perfect world I would go to college to pursue law, neuroscience or immunology. However, all paths would take years to achieve and start making money. On average, becoming an attorney takes seven years. Seven years without sufficient income, then I have to work my way up the corporate ladder so I can have a decent paying job. For context, when I researched this career in early 2023, I was also reading how many people were debating if six figures was still a sufficient salary due to the cost of living increase.

Since my plan was to attend Stanford, I knew living in California would take a nice paycheck. The situation is similar for immunology, yet I wouldn't start making actual money until my thirties, possibly late twenties if I graduated high school early. I knew the yearly salary of completing residency would be around fifty to sixty grand. While it's better than nothing, I worry about struggling financially in a different state and having to rely on my parents or an extra job. While I could pick a college closer to home with less expenses, I don't want to compromise on my dream. I know my parents would figure out the cost and extend themselves every way possible to make my plans come true, but they shouldn't have to, especially when it's not wholehearted my dream.

while i do not have the money to live in a new state for years and not make sufficient money, i do have the freedom to not compromise on my dreams.

there are many solutions to the dilemma, but i still see a compromise that isn't worth it.

Working extra jobs while balancing school and miss exciting new social interactions.

Attend a less expsenve college and miss my dream college.

the list can continue.

Bottom line:

I WILL ONLY COMPRISE FOR MY PASSIONS AND WHOLEHEARTED DREAMS.

You should, too.

iF bEcoMiNG A NEURosURGEoN is YoUR WhoLEhEARTEd dREAM, do iT.

If becoming the Vice President of Bank of America is your wholehearted dream, do it.

If becoming a rice farmer with 25 acres of land is your wholehearted dream, do it.

If becoming creative director at Givenchy is your wholehearted dream, do it.

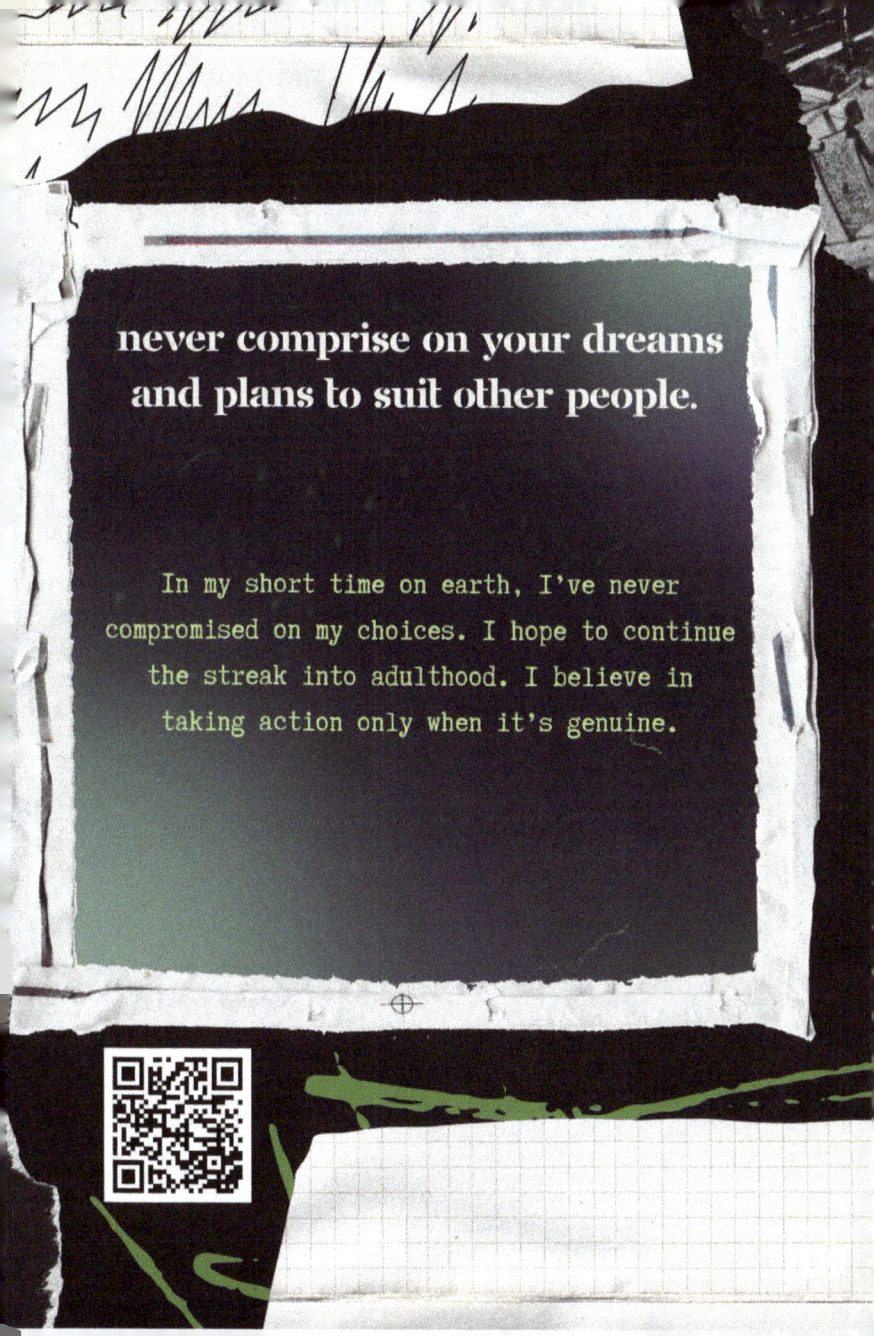

never comprise on your dreams and plans to suit other people.

In my short time on earth, I've never compromised on my choices. I hope to continue the streak into adulthood. I believe in taking action only when it's genuine.

SAFETY FIRST!

I am considered an inconvenience to society for something I can not control.

At age 2, I was diagnosed with a peanut and tree nut allergy. For those who don't know, a food allergy is when a person's immune systems mistakes the protein certain food to be harmful. When a person comes in contact with their food allergy (eating, touching), they experience an allergic reaction. An allergic reaction can start off mild, then escalate to anaphylaxis which can be fatal. Once I was diagnosed, my parent's life dramatically changed. Restaurants, family events, entertainment places (Chuck E Cheese, etc), parties and even brick and mortar school became dangerous. In fear of an anaphylactic reaction, my parents opted for virtual school and heavily controlled my environment. My parents quickly found out the world doesn't pay mind to people with food allergies, as if we are an inconvenience. I believe it's a lack of empathy and compassion to not accommodate a person's medical condition.

Fears and limitations surrounding my own food allergy made me yearn to create a space where food allergies are respected and welcomed. When I received the building, I was so excited to host my own events and workshops. I remember I hosted a Halloween Game Night. It was a free event where we served peanut and tree nut free food and invited guest to play games. The event lasted from 6:00 pm to 8:00 pm. I sat in the building with my parents for two hours, waiting for a soul to enter.

I see people rally and respect other serious medical conditions, but I contours wonder why food allergies are not as respected. I've read articles of allergic reactions occurring, and the public response is always negative. Seeing people comment about how people with food allergies should "stay inside" and how it's not the world's job to accommodate solidifies my feeling of being an inconvenience. While I should not let public opinion cloud my mind, I have experienced the miseducation, ignorance, and carelessness firsthand.

In April 2024, a female empowerment organization I worked with in the past asked me to be a part of their panel for an event they were hosting. I gladly said yes.

However, as soon as my cheeks turned upwards, they turned downwards.

The brunch was hosted at a trendy place in my city. Unfortunately, trendy didn't mean it was food allergy friendly. I couldn't eat at any restaurant in town, so I reluctantly accepted. Similar to when I attended brick-and-mortar school in fourth grade, I knew how to handle myself. However, a recommendation from my allergist or talks with my parents could not prepare me for this feeling. When brunch first started, the panel members and I conversated. It was great to be around like-minded females.

However, the style of the restaurant was buffet-like, and you would stand in line to order, then your food would come to you. Being that the place was trendy, it was filled with people. I was seated at the table, while the other guest waited in line. The wait was around 45 minutes long.

I was just there.

The organization booked the largest table, right in the center of the restaurant. I was the only one seated at the table and I was garnering strange looks from other people in the restaurant. The leader of organization didn't inform me the wait would be so long, so I patiently waited.

Yet, it didn't stop me from feeling
uncomfortable with being the only one in a
crowded restaurant not eating. However, I think
the part of the situation that bothered me the
most was when the organization leader told me:

"I'm allergic to shellfish, but I can still eat
here. I'm glad you were still able to attend,
despite your food allergy"

The first sentence completely baffled me. For
context, the restaurant did not serve peanuts, but
fried in peanut oil. I also know the restaurant
served food with shellfish. Personally, with the
organization leader having a shellfish allergy, I
didn't think it was right for her to eat there
knowing shellfish was served. I also found the first
sentence of her statement to be unnecessary and
shows how little people understand food allergies.

When trying to have empathy or show compassion to someone with a food allergy, show understanding in your actions, not just your words.

Once the food was served, the brunch was great. We talked and planned for the upcoming panel. I could tell all the women I was surrounded by were good hearted, just misinformed about food allergies.

Once the brunch was finished, I ate Whataburger and told my parents the encounter.

For a long time, my environment was controlled
and I knew what I could and couldn't do. My
parents and I didn't attend events because we
knew my food allergy would not be accommodated.

I enjoyed life from afar on roadtrips and
Sunday drives. I baked cakes and cookies in my
spare time. In a way, I forgot the feeling of
having a food allergy. The nervousness of being
in a new place, not knowing if something can
trigger you. The feeling of knowing you are the
only one not eating and thinking about what
other people think of you when they look in
your direction. The feeling of knowing the
people you are with do not understand and will
most likely try to discredit your allergy.

I could have skipped the brunch, but it might had meant missing the opportunity to be a panel member. The choice was mine and my parents were weary of letting me attend.

I persuaded them and thought I could "suck it up" like a true business woman.

HoWEVER, You cAN'T "sUcK Up" ThE FEELiNG oF bEiNG aN iNCoNVENiENCE aNd LiKE ThE WoRLd doEsN'T CaRE AbouT YouR LiFE ThREaTENiNG MEdiCaL coNdiTioN.

That encounter at brunch has solidified my mission in becoming a food allergy advocate, someone who speaks, provides solutions and calls out the misinformation and mistreatment of food allergies.

the

ai

CHAPTER

crazy thing, I manifested AI, Chat GPT and DALL-E as a chid. Crazier thing, I didn't want to use either software when it debuted.

As previously mentioned I'm writer who needs illustrations to publish her work. Yet, when I first learned about artificial intelligence (AI), I couldn't stand to hear the full sentence. I was infuriated. One day, I saw a segment on CBS News show how Chat GPT can write essays.

i, someone who enjoys writing essays, was flabbergasted.

"IT'S GOING TO TAKE AWAY ACADEMICS."

"CHILDREN WILL HAVE EMPTY BRAINS."

"THE AMERICAN LITERACY CRISIS WILL WORSEN."

Anytime AI was mentioned in news or media, my ears closed.

BLAH BLAH BLAH BLAH BLAH BLAH BLAH BLAH BLAH BLAH BLAH

A NEW TECHNOLOGY REPLACING WRITERS ??

my feelings about ai, a year ago compared to now are very hypocritical.

As children, we see science fiction in the movies. Even daydream about it. I always wished for a device to know what I'm thinking, to create a visual. Currently, AI is the closest tech we have to my idea.

SO WHY DIDN'T I WANT TO USE AI?

The simplest answer is fear and lack of understanding.

I feared AI Would take away what I love most: writing.

I feared AI would plunge society into brainless zombies.

I also didn't understand how AI operated.

AI needs humans and words to perform actions which leads me to the conclusion: writing is still needed.

RWTCLSP are valuable skills need to harness a valuable technology.

I first realized writing's key link to AI one night when I was experimenting. I was in a gloomy mood, the first cracks in my business started to show and my normal coping mechanism of baking didn't work.

SO, I REVISITED AN OLD LOVE:

my collection *OF* SOON TO BE
OFFICIALLY PUBLISHED
childhood stories

A collection of stories I wrote
throughout my childhood that begged
to become published. The only thing
missing were illustrations.

The design software I used was advertising their new AI image creator. It wasn't just desperation, the longing feeling of seeing your character come to life, but rather a realization.

This new technology can help me overcome the ultimate hurdle in publishing my writing.

I wasn't putting pride aside or casting all my stubbornness away, but instead maturing and evolving with technology.

I closed my eyes and envisioned the character I wanted AI to create. It didn't take long before my prompt was fully typed. I clicked the "generate" button hopefully.

(Am I really doing this?)

This is the part where confetti explodes, the sun shines and I tell you all my dreams came true.

not exactly.

The prompt I wrote, my vision and the AI output did not match. However, I revised my prompt by adding and taking away certain details. I also told AI which images I liked and didn't like.

LITTLE DID I KNOW TRAINING AI

I trained AI to create my vision accurately, and I did it all with the power of writing, and communication Skills.

In one evening, I learned something the media didn't scream about.

WRITING AND COMMUNICATION ARE TIMELESS AND WILL FOREVER REIGN SUPREME.

AI needs humons to tell it what to do, how to do it to recieve to receive the desired result.

Whether humans control AI by talking to it aloud or using descriptive prompts, communication and writing skills are needed.

Pivot,
Pivot!

"PIVOT, PIVOT"

is a very funny meme.

The phrase is also one of my mottos.

piv•ot
/ˈPIVəT/

NOUN   a shaft or pin on which something turns.

VERB   **1** turn on or as if on a pivot.

        2 (especially in a business context) completely change the way in which one does something.

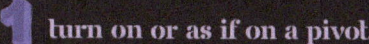

> Looking back on the first half of 2024, I'm glad the meme stuck in my head.

Around October 2023 was my first experience in pivoting. My original business plan of youth workshops, events and after school programs was not working. While I thought people needed more time to discover the business, my parents went to the drawing board. Together, we thought of a way to provide our services for free, to cater to the financial status of the community.

in the end, that direction didn't work either. still, the method of pivoting stuck with me.

Staring January 2024, I decided to pivot.
(again)

Once my inhabitance of the building was gone, I tried to bring my business to the online space. I tried my hand at workshops introducing AI to kids and selling AI art. I tried selling programs and courses to businesses. That didn't work either.

I DECIDED, IT WAS ME.

I let the unresponsive nature of people who did not support my business leave a stain on it.
A stain that made me question if the business could ever be successful.

So I gave it up, in favor of a new venture:

ME

After I decided to retreat to the drawing board and pivot, I came up with a new plan:

establish my presence on social media

A factor I believe hindered the success of my business. The same month, I became obsessed with marketing. I would watch videos and read articles about social media marketing for hours. In return, I decided to build my personal brand. I created social media accounts as a way to build my presence.

However, I caught a case of what I call:

"REFLECTION SYNDROME"

The videos I filmed in my room reflected not me, but the marketing content I consumed. Marketing is a mere interest of mine, but it's not who I am. My voice was being lost in a sea of bittersweetness as I clawed for a sign or clue to tell me if I was worthy of impacting people.

JUNE 2024

social media accounts are deleted

SELF CONFIDENCE IS NOW RESTORED

Something bigger than myself is in the works

As I write this, I have just published the first story in my mission to publish all of my childhood short stories.

i only have one social media account, under the name officially_halee, my media persona.

In a short time between January and June, I found myself. A switch has been flicked on in my brain and I understand. I understand that people don't just support the good because it's good. I understand plans fail and pivoting is a nessicty. I understand stumbling upon one flawed town doesn't mean I can't change the world. I have made a choice, to be a successful person. I also understand something very important:

TRENDS DON'T MAKE LEGENDS

PROVE THE ADULTS WRONG

you are productive

you do want to better yourself

you have goals

you have ambitions

you are motivated

you are respectful

you want to learn

you want to be successful

YEAR

was unlike anything I expected. Yet, it was one of the best years of my life. I learned so much and I'm glad I can share it with you all. This book is not intended to shame (or diss) anyone, but rather recall experiences I had that shaped my thinking, created questions and the lessons I learned.

It is a cliche, but the biggest theme this book represents is **when life gives your lemons, make lemonade.**

Life may seem unfair and your plans may be going awry, but as a teen (or tween!), you have the choice to keep going with your goals, plans and dreams.

You also have the choice to alter your goals, plans and dreams. Not to sound like a mature adult but, you have time! You're young! Life is going to happen and one failure doesn't mean your story is over,

(eVEN iF This oNE is)

ACCESS TO ALL THAT IS

13 THINGS

videos, free stuff and more!

DOING WHAT'S

SAYING

BE NO

ST

FOR YOU

SELF

LOVE

PUTTING

KNOWING HOW TO

YO LO

U VE

FIRST

YOURSELF

13 THINGS

MERch

Purchase the full
collection by scanning
the code with your
phone camera.

13

THI

NGS

www.ingramcontent.com/pod-product-compliance
Lightning Source LLC
Chambersburg PA
CBHW050442150626
46551CB00028B/1118

FROM ONE  year old

TO ALL THE TWEENS AND TEENS IN THE WORLD:

You will question who you are, what you're worth and if your dreams are possible.

People don't always clap for you when they should.

LiFE is TouGh.

I learned all of this at **13** years old when a big project of mine failed. I didn't have a book, or a friend to tell me one failure doesn't mean you can't be a successful teen. My parents kept my spirits high, but as a teenager you still question things. So, let's question together. In thirteen chapters you'll read about the lessons I learned, the questions I asked and most importantly, how I found the courage to try again.

$17.99
ISBN 979-8-990956-3-4
51799